Thomas John Capel

Great Britain and Rome

Or, Ought the Queen of England to Hold Diplomatic Relations with the

Sovereign Pontiff?

Thomas John Capel

Great Britain and Rome
Or, Ought the Queen of England to Hold Diplomatic Relations with the Sovereign Pontiff?

ISBN/EAN: 9783744773478

Printed in Europe, USA, Canada, Australia, Japan

Cover: Foto ©ninafisch / pixelio.de

More available books at **www.hansebooks.com**

GREAT BRITAIN AND ROME.

At the end of October last the 'Morning Post' announced in a short article that quasi-diplomatic relations were about to be re-established between England and Rome, and that Mr. Errington, M.P., had been deputed by the English Government to negotiate the matter with the Holy See. This statement was denied by a portion of the press, yet the 'Morning Post' has not only adhered to it, but also from time to time, and apparently with authority, added other statements, which furnish the public mind with sufficient ground for believing the original report. Since then the political atmosphere has been overcharged with rumours of negotiations concerning efforts which, it is said, are being made to secure the independence of the Pope. It is, therefore, not inopportune to ask the question, Ought the Queen of England to hold diplomatic relations with the Sovereign Pontiff? Those of the political school which opposed Catholic Emancipation, and which has opposed every subsequent measure brought forward with the view of extending to Roman Catholics the rights they have justly claimed; which has resisted, inch by inch, every concession of religious liberty to Roman Catholics; will consider the question hardly worthy of a response, and will instinctively say, Hold no communication with Rome—*Roma delenda est.* But, laying aside prejudice, let us bring the matter to the bar of reason

Limiting ourselves for the moment to its internal life, the British Empire numbers amongst its subjects no less than ten millions of Roman Catholics. They are to be found in masses in Ireland, Canada, Malta, and Gibraltar, as well as in the great centres of commerce and industry throughout Great Britain. They permeate the organisation of the Empire, taking part in most of the functions of the State, from those of members of the Privy Council or of Viceroy of India, to those of the lowest official under the Crown; and in the social order the positions they occupy extend from that of the first duke of the realm to that of the needy poor in the workhouse. Their well-being must necessarily be one factor in the well-being of the whole nation.

These Roman Catholic subjects, differing as they do in race, language, and political creed, are nevertheless one in mind and heart as regards religious belief and practice. Within the limits of the empire they are distributed into some 134 dioceses, ruled by 17 archbishops and 100 bishops, and they are served by at least 10,000 priests. They are possessed of schools for elementary and intermediate education; of colleges and universities; of charitable institutions of various kinds, managed by different religious orders and congregations, whose members are exclusively devoted for life to these special works; and all this system forms but a part of that mighty organisation which extends depends on the Roman Pontiff as centre and source of its religious life.

As recently as 1780 the law of this country made it felony in any Roman Catholic priest, and high treason in one who was a native of the kingdom, to teach the doctrines or to perform the rites of his Church. Forty-nine years of struggle from that date on the part of the Catholics of Ireland, England, and Scotland, together with the aid of liberal-minded statesmen, ended in the Emancipation Act of 1829. This Catholic Relief Bill, together with later enactments in the same just spirit of legislation, recognises as a fact the existence of the Catholic Church in the empire. Catholics are thus not merely tolerated but acknowledged by the law as a body of persons having certain essential and characteristic features; and though still excluded from the offices of Regent of the United Kingdom, Viceroy of Ireland, Lord Chancellor of England, Lord Keeper or Lords Commissioners of the Great Seal of Great Britain or Ireland, and Lord High Commissioner of the General Assembly of the Church of Scotland, they are considered eligible to every other appointment under the Crown. Further, the said relief Acts have allowed and enabled Roman Catholics to profess and practise their faith without let or hindrance, provided they violate no part of the law. And the distinctive feature of that faith, obedience to and communion with the Roman See, is very clearly admitted and recognised by the said Emancipation Act, 'being for his Majesty's subjects professing the ROMAN Catholic religion;' and also in the form of oath appointed and set forth by the Act to be used by ROMAN Catholics.

This is not the place to enter into the theological arguments or the historical testimony which can be adduced in favour of the central Catholic doctrine of the Supremacy of the Pope.[1] For the investigation of the question at present under consideration, it will suffice that the bearings of the doctrine should be fully seen; and this purpose will be attained by giving a clear statement of it.

Catholics hold that our Blessed Lord called into existence, and Himself directly fashioned, an organic body, a Corporation, known as the Church; that this Church is His kingdom *in* the world, but not *of* it; that to this Church was committed exclusively the guardianship of the Divine revelation which He had made known; that she alone has the right to judge of the meaning of such revelation and to propound it; that to her solely appertains the duty and privilege of dispensing the mysteries of God; and that she exists for a spiritual end—namely, the salvation of man and the glory of God. Catholics further hold that in the constitution of the Church, and as essential to that constitution, there exists a Sacerdotal, an Episcopal, and an Apostolic Power; that the Apostolic Power is concentrated, in all its plenitude, in the Pope, as the legitimate successor of St. Peter, on whom Christ conferred it. Catholics consequently hold the Pope to be supreme head of the Church, supreme priest, supreme legislator in ecclesiastical affairs, supreme judge in ecclesiastical causes, and supreme teacher in all matters of faith and morals. The Pope, then, (1) holds supreme power over the whole Church; (2) to him it belongs to convoke councils, to revise and to confirm their decrees; (3) to proclaim decrees for the whole Church in regard to discipline; (4) to decide authoritatively and infallibly in matters of faith and morals; (5) the Pope is the centre of the Catholic communion, separation from whom is separation from the Church ; (6) he has the final power of appointing bishops—the nomination of candidates by sovereigns, by the clergy, or by synods of bishops always being subject to his confirmation of their election ; (7) he has likewise the power of depriving bishops of their pastoral office and of accepting their resignation : in a word, the Pope has a mission extending over the whole earth, and embracing the whole moral and ecclesiastical order. All this is included in the Catholic doctrine of the Pope's Supremacy, and is fully covered by the decree of the Council of Florence, in the following words

Moreover, we define that the Holy Apostolic See and the Roman Bishop has the primacy over all the earth and that he is the successor of the Blessed Peter, the Prince of the Apostles, the true Vicar of Christ, the Head of the whole Church, and the Father and Teacher of all Christians ; and that to him in the person of the Blessed Peter was committed by our Lord Jesus Christ the full power of feeding, directing, and governing the Universal Church as it is contained in the Acts of General Councils and in the Sacred Canons.'

But not only does each Catholic believe this, he also personally feels the action of this supreme power in his own spiritual life. He is brought spiritually in contact with the Pope, and thus in a genuine and real sense calls the Pope *Holy Father*. For, believing as the Catholic does, that the Pope, to use the beautiful words of Cardinal Newman, ' like St. Peter, is the Vicar of his Lord. He can judge and he can acquit ; he can pardon and he can condemn ; he can command and he can permit ; he can forbid and he can punish. He has a supreme jurisdiction over the people of God. He can stop the ordinary course of sacramental mercies ; he can excommunicate from the ordinary grace of redemption, and he can remove again the ban which he has inflicted. It is the rule of Christ's providence that what His Vicar does in severity or in mercy upon earth He Himself confirms in Heaven'—believing all this, the individual Catholic knows that every absolution he receives, every sermon he hears preached, every indulgence he gains, every blessing in fact that comes to his soul through the ordinary channels of divine grace, is derived directly from his immediate priest or bishop, and ultimately from Christ's Vicegerent, the Pope, who from that reservoir of spiritual and divine authority and grace, entrusted to him by the incarnate Son of God, dispenses, through duly appointed ministers, the water of life to each individual soul in Holy Church.

From what we have said, it may easily be concluded that while Catholics regard the Pope as man, peccable man, standing as all others do in need of saving grace, they must yet have for him, on account of his high and unique office, singular reverence, devotion, and affection. We will again quote from the writings of Cardinal Newman, who has in powerful language expressed the sentiments of every true Catholic heart. 'What need I say more,' writes his Eminence, 'to measure our own duty to it (the Holy See), and to him who sits in it, than to say that in his administration of Christ's kingdom, in his religious acts, we must never oppose his will, or dispute his word, or criticise his policy, or shrink from his side? There are kings of the earth who have despotic authority, which their subjects obey indeed, but disown in their hearts. But we must never murmur at that absolute rule which the Sovereign Pontiff has over us, because it is given to him by Christ, and in obeying him we are obeying his Lord. We must never suffer ourselves to doubt that, in his government of the Church, he is guided by an intelligence more than

DIVINE ORIGIN OF CIVIL POWER. 11

human. His yoke is the yoke of Christ; *he* has the responsibility of his own acts, not we; and to *his Lord* must he render account, not to us. Even in secular matters it is ever safe to be on his side, dangerous to be on the side of his enemies. Our duty is not, indeed, to mix up Christ's Vicar with this or that party of men, because he in his high station is above all parties, but to look at his formal deeds, and to follow him whither he goeth, and never to desert him, however we may be tried, but to defend him at all hazards and against all comers, as a son would a father, and as a wife a husband, knowing that his cause is the cause of God. And so as regards his successors, if we live to see them; it is our duty to give *them* in like manner our dutiful allegiance and our unfeigned service, and to follow them also whithersoever they go, having that same confidence that each in his turn and in his own day will do God's work and will, which we felt in their predecessors, now taken away to their eternal reward.'

The theological reasons for the devotion of Catholics to the Pope would, as we have already observed, be out of place in this pamphlet, but what we have said is sufficient to show that the doctrine of the Pope's supremacy is the central belief of Catholics; for it they have joyfully suffered; for it they are proud to die, and persecution is powerless to eradicate from their hearts the conviction that the Pope is the spiritual and supreme Father of all the faithful.

Another truth equally held by Catholics is that all power is from God, and that every soul is bound to be subject to the higher powers as ordained of God, whether it be to the king, as excelling, or to governors as sent by him; and that those that resist purchase to themselves damnation. And they feel and believe that the Divine law which requires their obedience to the

Church also requires and regulates their obedience to the authority of earthly government. This authority, according to Catholic belief, is from God. The assertion that civil power emanates from the people is contrary to the Catholic faith. 'There is no power but from God,' says St. Paul, and our Holy Father Leo XIII. in his Encyclical,[1] '*Diuturnum*,' uses the following words: 'God is the natural and necessary principle of authority in civil government;' and again, 'The Church teaches that civil power comes from God,' and in the next paragraph declares that 'God is the fountain of all human authority,' and further on, that 'the origin of all power and dominion is derived from one and the same Creator and Lord of the Universe.' In other words, the Catholic faith teaches that civil power is not from the people ultimately. The people may choose any form of government they like, whether democracy, aristocracy, or monarchy, but their choice does not create the power, it only determines who is to hold and exercise this power, which God alone can give. It follows, therefore, that, as the authority of the ruler of the State is a certain communication of Divine power, obedience to such ruler within the limits of his legitimate authority is binding on conscience.

Again, God has established a third authority on earth. He, 'of whom all paternity is named in heaven and earth,' has been pleased divinely to institute the family, giving parents power and authority over their children, and exacting of children love, reverence, and obedience to their parents. The parental, like the civil, power is founded in the law of nature, and is re-asserted in the law of the Gospel.

The authority of the Church, the authority of the State, and the authority of the parent have all emanated

[1] The Encyclical is to be found as an appendix to this pamphlet.

from the same God; each has its own end to accomplish, each has its own circumscribed limits, each has within those circumscribed limits its own independence and its own prerogative. God's work of creation, of conservation, of sanctification, is continued respectively by the Family, the State, the Church. The Family rules the individual, the individual and families are subjected to the State, while under the spiritual rule of the Church are individuals, nations, and the whole human race. In the Divine economy these three concentric powers are able, and are intended to render each other in operation effective assistance. Working together harmoniously, they produce in the individual peace and happiness, and tend to the greatest general good.

The Church in her infancy lived under pagan emperors, and yet her teachers urged obedience to the civil power for conscience sake. 'Be ye subject,' says St. Peter, 'to every human creature for God's sake; whether it be to the king, as excelling, or to governors as sent by him for the punishment of evil doers, and for the praise of the good, for so is the will of God.' Shortly after Constantine had been converted and when the Church shone forth in her glory, St. Augustine said of her, the City of God : 'So[1] long as it lives like a captive and a stranger in the earthly city, though it has already received the promise of redemption and the gift of the Spirit as the earnest of it, it makes no scruple to obey the laws of the earthly city whereby things necessary for the maintenance of this mortal life are administered ; and thus, as this life is common to both cities, so there is a harmony between them in regard to what belongs to it.' And a little further on, St. Augustine adds: 'This heavenly city, then, while it sojourns on earth,

[1] *De Civitate Dei*, lxix. c. 17.

calls citizens out of all nations, and gathers together a society of pilgrims of all languages, not scrupling about diversities in the manners, laws, and institutions whereby earthly peace is secured and maintained, but recognising that, however various these are, they all tend to one and the same end of earthly peace. It therefore is so far from rescinding and abolishing these diversities that it even preserves and adopts them so long as no hindrance to the worship of the one true God is thus introduced.' Fourteen centuries and a half have passed since the Bishop of Hippo wrote those words, and to-day the City of God, stripped in great measure of earthly possessions, dwells in earthly cities, monarchical and republican, governed by pagan and Mussulman rulers, as well as in others under the sway of kings and governors professing different forms of Christianity ; to each of such potentates it renders obedience, recognising and proclaiming that 'God hath set a ruler over every nation,'[1] that 'the prince is the minister of God,'[2] and that we are to 'be subject of necessity, not only for wrath, but also for conscience sake.'[3] And the Pope, the Supreme Governor of this City of God on earth, addresses all other pastors of that city in his Encyclical of June 28, 1881, in these words: 'The Church of Christ indeed cannot be an object of suspicion to rulers, nor of hatred to the people ; for it urges rulers to follow justice, and in nothing to decline from their duty ; while at the same time it strengthens and in many ways supports their authority. All things that are of a civil nature the Church acknowledges and declares to be under the power and authority of the ruler ; and in those things, the judgment of which belongs for different reasons both to the sacred and to the civil power, the Church wishes that there should be harmony between

[1] Eccl. xvii. 14.   [2] Rom. xiii. 4.   [3] Rom. xiii. 3.

the two, so that injurious contests may be avoided. As to what regards the people, the Church has been established for the salvation of all men and has ever loved them as a mother.' In a previous part of the same Encyclical His Holiness says: 'There is no question here respecting forms of government, for there is no reason why the Church should not approve of the chief power being held by one man, or by more, provided only it be just, and that it tend to the common advantage. Wherefore, so long as justice be respected, the people are not hindered from choosing for themselves that form of government which suits best either their own disposition or the institutions and customs of their ancestors.'

To each of these powers, within its own appointed limits, Catholics hold that loyal conscientious obedience must be rendered. No human authority can bind conscience, unless such authority act in conformity with the law of God. In case, therefore, of conflict between these powers, the individual must follow the dictates of conscience; and must, where the matter is doubtful, turn to the spiritual authority for the final decision as to the *moral* lawfulness of an action. For the spiritual power exists in order to instruct individuals as well as societies of men in the law of God, and to judge of the morality and justice of all actions. In this way the spiritual power does exercise indirect action over civil power, and in this sense is superior to it, being also superior in its object, which is to lead men to eternal salvation. 'Politics, or that science which treats of the State, must necessarily, from its ethical character, present many points of contact with revealed truth. The principles on which it is based flow from the natural law. They can, therefore, never be in real contradiction with the precepts of Divine and positive law.

Hence the State, if it only remain true to its fundamental principles, must ever be in the completest harmony with the Church and Revelation. Now, so long as this harmony continues, the Church has neither call nor right to interfere with the State, for earthly politics do not fall within her direct jurisdiction. The moment, however, the State becomes unfaithful to its principles, and contravenes the Divine and positive law, that moment it is the Church's right and duty, as guardian of revealed truth, to interfere and to proclaim to the State the truths which it has ignored, and to condemn the erroneous maxims which it has adopted.'[1] Under such circumstances the Pope is the ultimate interpreter of the moral law; when a doubt arises concerning the moral rectitude of acts, even in the civil order, the final decision rests with the Pope.

Keeping these principles in mind, we may now give an answer to the question, 'Ought the Sovereign of Great Britain to hold diplomatic relations with the Sovereign Pontiff?'

II.

1. In virtue of the liberty granted by the Constitution of England, Roman Catholics, without any violation of the law of the land, acknowledge the Sovereign Pontiff to be the supreme fountain of spiritual and Divine authority on earth. Cardinals and archbishops, bishops, prelates, and priests—all commissioned officers of the Supreme Pontiff—exercise, in subjection to His Holiness, their spiritual authority in all parts of the British Empire. The government of the country and of the colonies is, necessarily, and in various ways, brought into official communication with these Papal pastors, and in some instances it gives salaries to these pastors for the

[1] Knox, *When does the Church speak infallibly?* p. 70.

work they do. Each one of these pastors receives his mission or jurisdiction, directly or indirectly, from the Pope. Such jurisdiction is limited as to place and duration, and can be withdrawn or withheld by the will of the power that gives it. Now what can be more inconsistent than readily to receive and recognise these lieutenants, many of whom are foreigners of different nations, and yet to refuse to hold intercourse with their chief himself? A country that ran wild in paying honour to the Shah of Persia and to the Ottoman Sultan, and will probably act in like manner towards Cetewayo, when his ex-Majesty arrives amongst us, declines to enter into relations with the Head of the oldest and most venerable of European kingdoms, with the Father of Christian civilisation, the Sovereign who rules the powerful kingdom of Christ.

Not only is this attitude towards the Sovereign Pontiff inconsistent, but it deeply wounds Roman Catholics, who see in it covert distrust and suspicion, and even actual insult. They love the Pope with filial affection, and feel themselves injured in his person. The recognition of the Sovereign Pontiff by the British Government would be an honour conferred on each individual Catholic in the empire, would create in each heart a new sense of personal dignity, and would furnish to each a new motive for devotion to the Crown.

For special reasons over and above the fact of the general participation of England in the civilisation produced by Roman Catholicism, the memories of Papal influence ought to be dear to Englishmen. The very life of the English nation was from its birth, and for nine hundred years of its existence, nurtured and moulded by the wisdom, the power, and the love of the Holy See. It was Pope Gregory VII. who sent the Roman monk Augustine to England, to impart to our

B

pagan ancestors the ight of Christianity. Half a century later, in 668, another Pope, by name Vitalian, sent the Greek monk Theodore, who organised the Episcopate and gave to the Church in England the outward episcopal and parochial form which the Anglican Communion retains even to this day. So solid were the fruits of Archbishop Theodore's labours, that 'in a single century England became known to Christendom as a fountain of light, as a land of learned men, of devout and unwearied missions, of strong, rich, and pious kings.'[1] His work not only tended to the spiritual well-being of the country, but also gave an impulse to national unity, for, as Green says, ' in his arrangement of dioceses, and the way in which he grouped them round the See of Canterbury, in his national synods and ecclesiastical canons, Theodore did, unconsciously, a political work. . . . The policy of Theodore clothed with a sacred form, and surrounded with Divine sanctions, a unity which as yet rested on no basis but the sword. The single throne of the one primate at Canterbury accustomed men's minds to the thought of a single throne for their one temporal over-lord. The regular subordination of priest to bishop, of bishop to primate, in the administration of the Church, supplied a mould on which the civil organisation of the State quietly shaped itself. Above all, the councils gathered by Theodore were the first of our national gatherings for general legislation. . . . The synods which Theodore convened as religiously representative of the whole English nation led the way by their example to our national parliament. The canons which these synods enacted led the way to a national system of law.'[2]

The Popes, in their wisdom, almost always sent

---

[1] Stubbs, *Const. Hist.*, vol. i. p. 251.
[2] *Hist. of English People*, vol. i. pp. 58, 59.

monks in the first instance as missionaries to our country, and so the different missionary stations, the bishops' houses, and the houses of the clergy, were either monasteries or fashioned on the form of the monasteries, and enjoyed their rights, privileges, and immunities. 'The monastic system,' to use the words of Stubbs, ' did its work well, and that a most important one for the time. It colonised the country by means of missions, furnished the supply of teachers in districts too poor and too thinly peopled to provide for their own clergy, and in a manner levelled and equalised the country for parochial administration.'[1] And so the Church of our Anglo-Saxon forefathers grew and prospered and silently moulded the solid form of the nation under the wise, active, and centralised power of the Holy See. 'The unity of the Church in England,' says Stubbs, ' was the pattern for the unity of the State; the cohesion of the Church was for ages the substitute for the cohesion which the divided nation was otherwise unable to realise. Strong in its own conformation it was more than a match for the despotic rule of such men as Offa, and was the guardian of liberties as well as the defence of the oppressed. . . . The ecclesiastical and the national spirit thus growing into one another supplied something at least of that strong passive power which (later) the Norman despotism was unable to break. The churches were schools and nurseries of patriots; depositories of old traditional glories and the refuge of the persecuted. . . . The unity of the Church was in the early period the only working unity; and its liberty in the evil days that followed the only form in which the traditions of the ancient freedom lingered. It was again to be the tie between the conquered and the conquerors; to give to the oppressed a hold on the

[1] Stubbs, vol. i. p. 255.

conscience of the despot; to win new liberties and revive the old; to unite Norman and Englishman in the resistance to tyrants, and educate the growing nation for its distant destiny as the teacher and herald of freedom to all the world.'[1]

A sacred attraction drew some of the greatest of the English kings to Rome. Ina, after laying the foundations of English law, resigned his crown in 728, and, having released his subjects from their allegiance, went to the tombs of the Apostles Peter and Paul to watch and pray, and ended his days in the calm seclusion of the monastic homes of the Holy City. In 853 Alfred was sent as a boy to Rome, and there he learned at the feet of Pope Leo IV. the principles of piety and of wisdom, and received from the hands of the Pontiff the Sacrament of Confirmation, and the royal unction before he began the great work of civilisation in England. From the tombs of the Apostles King Canute addressed to Egilnoth, Archbishop of Canterbury, the memorable letter wherein he strove to reverse whatever might have been unjust in the policy of his reign.

During that momentous period when England was really becoming England; while the conquered race was still subject to the proud, cruel Norman; and Saxons, Danes, and Normans had yet to be fused into a nation which should be one by blood, by language, and by constitution, the Roman Catholic Church did her work right nobly. By her Papal legates and her archbishops she won and preserved the liberties of the Church, which were at once restraints on the royal power and advantages for the people; the names of Lanfranc and St. Anselm recall the efforts made by these two great archbishops, with the aid of the abbots and monks and the support of the authority of the

[1] Stubbs, vol. i. pp. 280, 281.

Holy See, to vindicate the liberties of the people against the encroachments of royal tyranny.

Magna Charta, won by the barons and the people headed by Archbishop Langton, was the first great public act of the nation when it had realised its own unity after the amalgamation of the Norman and the English races. Its first article secured the liberty of the Church, 'quod Anglicana Ecclesia libera sit'—a liberty from the absolutism of the sovereign, not from the control of the Pope. But the same ecclesiastical hands that drew up the charter securing the freedom of the Church, carefully fenced round with provisions the rights of freeholders.[1] From the date of Magna Charta onwards till the rupture with Rome in the reign of Henry VIII. the Church took a leading part in all the important measures which agitated England. She exercised justice and charity in regard to the people, defended the oppressed, and by her influence brought about the liberation of those who were in the ignominious bondage of villeinage, and mitigated the asperities of feudalism.

Representative assemblies, municipalities, guilds, public schools, universities, and charitable institutions all owe their birth or their development to the energy of the Roman Church, to which we must also ascribe the glories of our architecture and the English literature of the middle ages.

No wonder that the English people loved the Church and her Sovereign Pontiff. There were, it is true, at times conflicts with Rome, and sundry Acts in the Statute Book bear evidence that the nation resisted claims made by some of the Popes to action in the civil affairs of the country, to certain revenues, to the appointment of foreigners to benefices, and the like.

[1] Stubbs, *Const. Hist.*, vol. i p. 597.

Such claims, let it be borne in mind, sprang, not from the Divine and essential power of the Papacy, but from the civil position and rights created by the nations of Europe, and conferred by them on the Sovereign Pontiff in the Middle Ages at a time when Feudalism was the governing spirit, and the Pope was not only the divinely appointed Head of the Church, but also the unanimously appointed Head of Christendom. The English people knew how to separate the Spiritual from the Temporal Authority of the Pope, and, while questioning some of the feudal rights of the latter, rendered dutiful obedience to the former. It was by no act of theirs that the authority of Rome was repudiated in the reign of Henry VIII. The wealth of the monasteries and the immunities and privileges of the clergy had indeed excited the jealousy of some men and the indignation of others; still the heart of the nation was sincerely attached to the Holy See. 'An historian (Burnet), whose bias was not unfavourable to Protestantism, confesses,' says Hallam, 'that all endeavours were too weak to overcome the aversion of the people towards reformation, and even intimates that German troops were sent from Calais on account of the bigotry with which the bulk of the nation adhered to the old superstition. This is somewhat an humiliating admission that the Protestant faith was imposed upon our ancestors by a foreign army [1]

The Tudors, for political purposes, robbed the people of their cherished inheritance, the Catholic religion. The separation from Rome was at the outset an individual act inspired by Cromwell; the divorce of Queen Catherine was but a pretext; the real purpose was to make the sovereign absolute. 'What the first of the Tudors,' to quote the words of Green, 'had done

[1] Hallam, *Const. Hist.*, vol. i. p. 92.

for the political independence of the kingdom, the second was to do for its ecclesiastical independence. . . . The last check on royal absolutism which had survived the Wars of the Roses, lay in the wealth, the independent synods and jurisdiction and claims of the Church; and for the success of the new policy it was necessary to reduce the great ecclesiastical body to a mere department of the State in which all authority should flow from the sovereign alone, his will be the only law, his decision the only test of truth.'[1] The consequent immediate injury inflicted on the nation at large and on the liberty of the people is amply witnessed by the page of England's history under the dictatorship of the Tudors and the despotism of the Stuarts. Englishmen with a remembrance of the lasting benefits received by their country through the influence and intervention of Rome ought, on the ground of gratitude, to greet with pleasure the renewal of diplomatic relations with the Sovereign Pontiff; and this apart from the honour of holding communications with the most venerable and most venerated of earthly sovereigns and the organ of the greatest spiritual power in the world.

2. The Pope claims no right of action, and has no wish to take part, in the civil affairs of the nation; he asks not for union with the State, nor for the aid of the civil power to enforce his commands. All that he desires is freedom for the development of every resource of the Church for the religious, moral, and intellectual progress and perfection of her children; and in those things, the judgment of which 'belongs, for different reasons, both to the sacred and the civil power, the Pope wishes that there should be harmony between the two, so that injurious contests may be avoided.' The

---

[1] Green, *Hist. of English People*, vol. ii. p. 152.

Holy Father presents himself as the teacher of morals, as the supporter of justice and the upholder of authority.

In the exercise of his authority as Supreme Ruler of the Church, it is needed that the Pope should be in possession of the most reliable and impartial information regarding the spiritual condition of his subjects in every part of the world, and that he should be thoroughly acquainted with the dispositions and the attitude of the civil power to which his subjects owe their allegiance in temporal matters. But how can such information be obtained better than by the actual residence of a representative of the Pope in each country, a representative superior to all local or diocesan interest, and having that access to reliable sources of knowledge afforded by a recognised diplomatic position?

And on the other hand, inasmuch as Catholics are bound to render conscientious obedience to the temporal authority under which they live, in all things within the legitimate scope of that authority, and yet cannot obey any human law that is against conscience and in opposition to the law of God, it is of paramount importance, in view of the interests of Catholic subjects, that each State should be aware of the existence and of the extent of the spiritual authority.

Mutual understanding in regard to these subjects; frank, loyal communication between the Pope and the civil government, would in many questions, such as national education, marriage, and the like, be of incalculable value—indeed of absolute necessity where a contract is to be entered into by the Catholic body. Grievances would frequently be removed at their first appearance; measures which would necessarily prove ineffectual would not be put forward; reverence for law and authority would be increased by the knowledge that perfect accord existed between the heads of spiritual and civil authority.

These considerations alone seem sufficient to prove the importance and expediency of holding diplomatic relations with Rome. But when we also bear in mind that every bishop in his diocese, and in a lesser degree every priest exercising jurisdiction, is a centre of genuine and living influence, in virtue of his sacred character and of his pastoral office, the importance, we might almost say the necessity, of such relations becomes yet more evident.

Over and above the general reasons which result from the great principles we have endeavoured to establish, there are in the constitution and circumstances of the British Empire motives which might well induce our Government to look on relations with the Sovereign Pontiff as most conducive to imperial integrity and prosperity. We do not pretend to say whether events will or will not justify the predictions of those politicians who believe that the shores of the Mediterranean will be the scene of the next great struggle among the nations; but in any case it is surely of the last importance to England that the Catholic bishops and priests of Gibraltar and Malta be loyal to her Crown. And if we turn to Canada, it requires but little penetration to see the ills that might occur should the Catholic clergy waver in their allegiance. There are many cases in which the Spiritual Ruler might without any sacrifice of the liberties of the Church act in harmony with the earthly authority, and *cæteris paribus* might appoint to influential ecclesiastical posts men whose loyalty was undoubted.

Again, the Empire has a grave responsibility in regard to its heathen subjects, and England must be credited with the wish to bring them under the influences of Christianity. In India Catholic missionaries, though beset by poverty and without any special support, are a strongly-organised body, and are doing a grand and glorious work. This work might be extended and promoted in a manner worthy of the power and the providential destiny of the British Empire were there a clear understanding and an intimate connection between England and the Pope.

Catholics see in the Pope only the Vicar of Christ, a loving Father, to whom they render childlike affection, forgetting of what nation he is; but it is objected by Protestants that the Pope is a foreigner, and that we cannot permit the interference of any foreigner in our domestic concerns. England has ever regarded the foreigner with suspicion, and has, not without reason, constantly resented any semblance of foreign interference in the civil affairs of the country. But the Pope specially disclaims any interference in purely civil affairs, and is concerned with religion alone. It must be remembered that religion and science are not like practical politics; they belong to no special country, and are not identified with any nationality. A nation may pride itself on the scientific men it has produced and nurtured, but science itself is cosmopolitan. So it is with religion. If we are to reject the moral and religious influence of the Pope because he may be a foreigner, we might on the same ground reject St. Peter, St. Paul, the writers of the Scriptures and the rest of the Apostles. Salvation indeed is of the Jew. Had King Ethelbert so treated St. Augustine when he as a *foreigner* came from the Roman Pontiff to Christianise England, we might now have been worshipping Woden and Thor, the heathen gods of our forefathers. It would doubtless have been flattering to our exclusive sensitiveness to have had an English Apostle to ourselves. However, it has been otherwise ordained. Christianity and many other great gifts have come to us through the foreigner.

Insular prejudice ought, at least in an age of such boasted progress, to give place to common sense. The Pope is a power, and the greatest power on earth. Men may not like him, but they cannot ignore him. In some way or other, communication has always been held by this country with the Holy See, whatever political party has been at the helm of affairs. Instead of doing this in a secret, makeshift, and therefore un-English manner, why should not a great nation like ours communicate openly and frankly with the Sovereign Pontiff, from whom we need fear no interference with the civil power, and whose influence and teaching can only confer great and lasting benefits on our people?

The Englishman's natural suspicion of the foreigner might make the politicians of Europe understand why Catholics assert so persistently that the Pope ought to be the subject of no sovereign, and, as it were, the member of no nation; why they feel that when he exercises his office there should be no room for even a suspicion of alien influence, and consequently maintain that he should have an evidently independent place of abode whither in times of peace or of war there can be the most unfettered access. It is strange that Italy even in its own interests should not realize this principle. Favoured by God, who has chosen Rome for the seat of His Vicar, Italy ought to be the first to remove from Catholics in every part of the world any ground of apprehension or distrust regarding the perfect freedom of action of the Pope; Italy should remember that she has not a monopoly of the Papacy. The good-will of all Catholics and the constant commerce with all that is greatest and noblest on earth, together with the consequent material advantages, might well be deemed an ample recompense for any sacrifice by which the complete temporal independence of the Sovereign Pontiff could be secured.

3. But it is urged that this recognition of the Pope is an infringement of the Royal Supremacy. Let no such false cry be raised. The supremacy of the sovereign, according to the law of the land, is two-fold; being at once civil or temporal, and spiritual or ecclesiastical. The temporal or civil supremacy of the Crown is commensurate with the Empire, and is owned by the three hundred and three millions of human beings under British rule. But the case is widely different in regard to the spiritual or ecclesiastical supremacy. This latter is admitted by but a small proportion of British subjects. The Buddhists and Mussulmans do not acknowledge it; and even among those who worship the one true and living God, Jews and Greeks, Quakers and Presbyterians, together with Nonconformists of every shade, do not profess obedience to the Crown in their spiritual concerns. Episcopalians alone, and of Episcopalians only those who belong to the Established Church of England, and are not advanced Ritualists—at most, not more than twenty millions, or one-fifteenth part of the population of the empire—allow that the sovereign is 'the only supreme governor of this realm and of all other Her Highness's dominions and countries, as well in all spiritual or ecclesiastical things or causes as temporal.' Roman Catholics do not, and cannot, admit the spiritual supremacy. By the Emancipation Act of 1829 they were liberated from the necessity of acknowledging it. They willingly and joyfully admit the civil supremacy; they render loyal obedience to the Crown from the highest of motives, recognising that its authority comes from God; with

honest pride they consider themselves to be second to none in devotion and loyalty.

Diplomatic relations with the Sovereign Pontiff would not then in the least degree interfere with the Queen's civil supremacy; on the contrary, the gratitude which Catholics would feel for the respect shown to their Supreme Pastor would furnish a fresh and powerful motive for their loyalty.

Our subject may be elucidated by an illustration drawn from certain acts of Royal Supremacy. In 1842, Her Majesty Queen Victoria, by letters patent, erected the Anglican Bishopric of Jerusalem, which is beyond the limit of her dominions. And in like manner other missionary bishoprics — Whitaker gives a list of ten—have been created by the royal authority of England in different countries ruled by other sovereigns. The Anglican Bishop of Gibraltar, in virtue of royal authority, holds and exercises a roving jurisdiction on the sea-board of countries around the Mediterranean, penetrating even to Rome itself. And similarly, by virtue of the same royal authority, the Archbishop of Canterbury exercises pastoral care over the Anglican communities scattered through northern and central Europe. There is no need here to inquire how far these arrangements may be compatible with the canonical decrees of the earliest General Council. The advisers of her Majesty and the law officers of the Crown would doubtless justify all such actions by reference to the Act 5 Vict. cap. 6, whereby the Archbishops of Canterbury and York may consecrate British subjects or foreigners to be bishops in foreign countries, and declares that such 'bishops so consecrated may exercise, within such limits as may from time to time be assigned for that purpose in such foreign countries, by Her Majesty, *spiritual jurisdiction* over the ministers of

British congregations of the United Church of England and Ireland, and over such other Protestant congregations as may be desirous of placing themselves under their authority.' It is expressly enacted that it shall not be required of such of these bishops 'as may be subjects or citizens of any foreign kingdom or state to take the oaths of allegiance and supremacy.' In other words, it would be said Her Majesty does her best to supply the spiritual wants of Anglicans abiding in foreign lands, be they her subjects or not. It may be reasonably asked, why, then, complain if the Pope acts similarly with regard to Catholics?

In the relations of the Sovereign Pontiff with Catholics of all nations His Holiness claims, by Divine right, submission merely to his spiritual authority. Even when there was a question of re-establishing the Roman Church in England in the reign of Queen Mary, the Pope asked nothing more. Commenting on the moderate character of the comprehensive bill framed by a joint committee of Lords and Commons in 1555 to effect this re-establishment, Lingard says: 'Most readers have very confused and incorrect notions of the jurisdiction which the Pontiff, in virtue of his supremacy, claimed to exercise within the realm. From this Act and the statutes which it repeals it follows that that jurisdiction was comprised under the following heads: (1) He was acknowledged as chief bishop of the Christian Church, with authority to reform and redress heresies, errors, and abuses within the same. (2) To him belonged the institution or confirmation of bishops elect. (3) He could grant to clergymen licence of non-residence and permission to hold more than one benefice with cure of souls. (4) He dispensed with the canonical impediments of matrimony; and (5) He received appeals from the spiritual courts.'[1] Evidently, then, the Pope had

[1] Lingard, *History of England*, vol. iv. p. 343, *note*.

no wish to interfere with the civil supremacy of the Crown.

In 1814, before the Congress of Vienna, that great statesman Cardinal Gonsalvi was in London, and, as he has himself recorded, was treated by the Prince Regent (afterwards George IV.) and many members of the aristocracy with every kind of respectful and amicable consideration. Pope Pius VII. writes in these words to His Eminence, instructing him as to the line of action he was to pursue: 'You are not merely charged with an important diplomatic mission, you are also the representative of the Vicar of Jesus Christ on earth. And for this reason we charge you to have the heart of a father for the poor English and Irish Catholics, who for centuries and from generation to generation have suffered in their property, in their liberty, and in their rights that they might remain faithful to the ancient faith of their fathers. You are the first cardinal who, since the reign of Elizabeth, has obtained leave to tread the soil of Great Britain. This privilege lays an obligation on us, and we ought not to close our ears to the cry of the persecuted. There is not, then, need to tell you what the Church expects of you. We know you sufficiently to trust that you will, with moderation and prudence, turn to account the present exceptional opportunity. Precipitate nothing, but neglect nothing that may soften the lot of the Catholics. By a mercy, for which we ought to thank Heaven, the Prince Regent overwhelms you with consideration and entertains a singular esteem for you. Try and beget in his heart the desire to be just towards subjects who have never failed in their duties as citizens, and you will see that this small grain of mustard-seed will bear abundant fruit. Sow, sow always; the reaper alone will by-and-by know the number of the sheaves.'[1] In all this there is not even a shadow of interference with the civil power.

It must be within the memory of many who may read this pamphlet that in 1850, when Pius IX. of blessed memory erected the Catholic Hierarchy in England, the cry of 'the royal supremacy in danger' was raised from pulpit and platform, in Parliament and by the press. A wave of 'no Popery' prejudice swept over the country, aroused ill-will and persecution, and precipitated hostile legislation. Thirty years have passed, and of the prophecies then so confidently uttered how many have been realised? how far have Catholics been wanting in allegiance? have they tried to disturb the Protestant settlement? or disputed the right of the present reigning family to the Crown? Those who boldly asserted that calamities would follow the establishment of the Hierarchy have lived to see their error, and the course of events has proved the truth of the great-minded Cardinal Wiseman's words: 'Time will disperse the mist and show the transaction in the true light.' For Catholics, from being a mere collection of individuals, have become a body politic, enjoying a more complete ecclesiastical and spiritual regimen; they have built churches, founded schools, and established charitable institutions of every kind. They have come forth from the nooks and corners where they lived isolated and timorous, and have commingled and identified themselves with their Protestant countrymen, in the general life of the nation, participating in its joys and its sorrows, and co-operating in its labours of philanthropy. The Crimean campaign, the Indian mutiny, the wars in Afghanistan and at the Cape, each bears witness to the loyalty and the courage of her Majesty's Catholic subjects. The establishment of the hierarchy gave new

[1] *Mémoires du Card. Gonsalvi*, vol. i. p. 82.

strength to Catholic patriotism. Hearts and lips that pray publicly Sunday after Sunday at Holy Mass that God would grant the Pope 'to benefit those over whom he is placed by word and example, that with the flock entrusted to him he may arrive at everlasting life,' the same hearts and lips after Holy Mass, make petition for their sovereign in these words: 'that Thy servant Victoria our Queen, who, by Thy mercy, has undertaken the government of the kingdom, may also receive an increase of all virtues, with which, being adorned as it becomes her, she may be enabled to avoid the monsters of vice and come to Thee well pleasing in Thy sight.'

4. The proposed communications with Rome are looked upon by other opponents as a result of the helplessness of the Government, in face of the present deplorable state of things in Ireland. It is hoped, they say, that Rome may exercise a spiritual 'dragooning' to do what the Coercion Act has failed to accomplish, and that the Irish priesthood may be employed to aid the Irish police. The grave and important question of the hour involved in this objection will necessitate and, it is hoped, justify a trespass on the reader's attention, which, under other circumstances, would with some reason be regarded as an irrelevant digression. It may, or may not, be true that the Ministry has sought the aid of the Holy See, but it shows an utter ignorance of Rome and of Rome's ways to imagine for a moment that the Pope will supply a spiritual police force to assist England in the government of Ireland, unless indeed the name of 'spiritual dragooning' is to be applied to any power by which the moral law is inculcated and upheld. The Church is made up of all nations, and tribes, and peoples, and tongues, but it is no part of her office to efface nationalities, or to suppress just national aspira-

tions. Her duty is to instruct men in justice and truth, and to dispense to them the bread of life. She has to urge men, by supernatural motives, to the accomplishment of duty, and the only sanctions she proclaims are those of the Divine law. The Sovereign Pontiff, therefore, can and does, with all the weight of his supreme authority, inculcate on the Catholics of Ireland a strict observance of the moral law, in all its bearings on obedience to law and authority, on respect for life and property, on forgiveness of injustice and injury, and everything that is comprised in our duty to man and to God. But His Holiness will never strive to stifle a legitimate craving of a much-suffering people for justice or remedial legislation.

England, by a system contrary to that pursued in other parts of her empire, has long tried to govern Ireland without regard to the character of the people and of their wants. They have cried for bread, and a stone has been offered them; they have asked for a fish, and have received a serpent. Measures based upon the individual theories of English statesmen of both political parties have at different times become legislative enactments for Ireland, and when such enactments have not been accepted, compulsory means have been taken to enforce them. No doubt this has very frequently been done with the best intentions in the world; but such good intentions cannot do away with the deplorable fact that the English Government has had in view, not the actual interests of the people, but what it believed ought to be their interests, and has given, not what the people really need, but what it thinks they ought to need.

And further, even in according that which Ireland has justly claimed, England has acted as if each concession were wrenched from her. Everything has been obtained by agitation, and it would seem that nothing can be obtained otherwise. The Irish people believe that if they agitate they will win; and this belief produces the worst political demoralisation. Adventurers who have nothing to lose but everything to gain find a ready hearing from a sensitive people, wounded to the very quick, and ready in their desperate misery to grasp at the shadow of hope, and to rely on any 'will-o'-the wisp' which leads them onwards.

The system of government tried has brought its inevitable consequences. Now that a remedial measure of the greatest importance has become the law of the land, it cannot obtain a fair trial. The venerable Hierarchy of Ireland, the archbishops and bishops assembled at Maynooth, declared that 'the new Land Act was a great benefit to the tenant class, and a large instalment of justice, for which the gratitude of the country was due to Mr. Gladstone and his Government, and all who helped to carry the measure through Parliament;' and they 'earnestly exhorted their flocks to avail themselves of the advantages derivable from the Act, believing that if rightly used it will bring present substantial benefit, and help them to obtain the rights, social and political, which they justly claim.' This advice has been neglected, and a 'no rent' cry has been raised; outrages on man and beast are frequent; honest men are seduced from duty or terrified by the fear of midnight murder; the well-disposed are incited to agrarian crime and flagrant dishonesty; and a state of anarchy prevails unworthy of Christians and of men. Unfortunately the remembrance of a past scarcely more than half a century gone by is easily brought back by designing persons to the mind of a highly imaginative people. Violence and crime ensue; 'but the guilt when the account is made up does not lie entirely with the poor wretch who is called the criminal.'

The agitation is widespread, it is in some measure kept alive by influences from without, and is participated in by men who seem to hesitate before no crime. It is not likely to burn itself out, nor, indeed, would this be a satisfactory way of ending the agitation. Authority must be respected, and law must be obeyed. Once and for all, why not strive to direct the movement into the hands of responsible and trustworthy leaders of the people? Why not seek the aid of the Roman Catholic clergy, for instance, by encouraging in every diocese, or even in every agricultural parish, the formation of committees, under the direction of the parish priests, the chairmen of such committees to be delegates under the bishops, to watch over and uphold the interests both of tenants and landlords. In this way the people would be led by safe and conscientious counsellors, a strong moral organisation would be created, a serious check would be given to evil-doers, to political adventurers, to unscrupulous agitators, and a fair trial might yet be given to the Land Act. Such a line of procedure would soon allow the liberation of the 'suspects,' and end the need for coercion, and for the present army of occupation.

Generally speaking, the interference of the clergy in politics is to be deplored and discouraged. Still priests, like other men, must have patriotism, and when they have suffered political wrongs with their people, and have been driven *nolens volens* into the position of political leaders, as has been the case in Ireland, then is it laudable for them corporately to take their part when a crisis like the present exists.

To ignore and not use such an influential factor for pacifying Ireland merely because it is Catholic would be to continue the unfortunate and destructive policy which England has for three centuries pursued towards the Sister Isle. Catholicism and the Catholic priesthood are the dearest treasures of the Irish heart, and yet every effort has been made to sever priest and people and to destroy their Faith. Lest I should seem to exaggerate, I will not use my own words, but cite those of one who was neither English nor Irish, but by birth, by education, and by residence an American, the late Mr. O. S. Brownson, a careful observer, who had many opportunities of knowing, and was a clear, outspoken writer. He says in his 'Review' for 1857, page 39: 'Catholic Ireland has been governed as a conquered country, and governed, too, by Protestants. The government for 300 years has been Protestant, and till within the last quarter of a century has done all in its power to trammel the Catholic religion and to debase and degrade the Catholic population. It deprived Catholics of all political power; it robbed them of all their churches, schools, and seminaries, outlawed their religion, hunted down their clergy as wild beasts, and prohibited by heavy penalties all education by Catholics. It seized all the revenues of the Church, confiscated the estates of Catholic proprietors, even prohibited Catholics from acquiring landed property or owning a horse of more than five pounds value. In a word, the Protestant Government, aided by a Protestant faction in Ireland, far worse than the Government itself, has during three hundred years done all in its power to impoverish, to debase, and brutalise the Catholic population.' And later on in the same article Brownson says: 'What has during these 300 years sustained the Catholic Irish and saved them from utter moral debasement and degradation? How have they been able to preserve one of the finest national characters in the world, and to give to the humblest shieling a dignity and moral grandeur which not one of England's proudest palaces can surpass? No man can for one moment doubt that it has been the Catholic religion, the Catholic faith, the Catholic Church.'

The *fons et origo* of the misery of English misrule in Ireland during the past three centuries is here honestly but somewhat bluntly stated. The Irish are intensely Catholic, and their religion is tinged by their nationality. Their priests are, generally speaking, taken from the people, and have never, as in some other countries, sided with a governing oppressing class; on the contrary, they have from circumstances constantly been the mouthpiece of the people's wrongs, and the champions of the people's liberties. Hence the people are bound to their priests by ties of exceptional love, reverence, and obedience. The living tenacity of faith, for which the Irish will freely sacrifice their all, is well known throughout the world.

Since the beginning of this century they have out of their poverty spent no less than 4,868,860*l*. in the erection of churches,[1] schools, convents, and seminaries, and this over and above the daily support of the Church throughout Ireland, while their zeal has led them to contribute to the spread of the Faith in other countries. Since 1838 they have given 149,124*l*. to the Society for the Propagation of the Faith, and they have sent forth more than a thousand priests to evangelise different parts of the world. Ireland's sons and daughters have founded most of the Catholic missions in the large towns of England; the pence of the Irish have mainly built and supported our churches and schools; more than a third of the priests working in England are of Irish blood. The efficient labour of Catholic elementary education in Great Britain is borne by a body of masters and mistresses, two-thirds of the former and half of the latter

[1] See Malone's *Church History of Ireland*, Preface.

being Irish. Sacrifices and deeds like these prove the value of the heavenly treasure of Catholic faith to the heart of the Irish nation.

It might have been expected that wise statesmanship would strive to take advantage of the moral power of such Faith; that it would show respect to the sacred convictions of such a people, and would endeavour to draw yet closer the bonds which unite it to its pastors; that those pastors would be given every assistance in finding the best possible education not only at home, which is done at Maynooth, but also in foreign Catholic lands. And in questions concerning the vital interests of the people, prudent statesmen might have been expected to seek aid from the knowledge, the experience, and the responsible influence of these pastors when legislating for the people. But by some singular perversity the English Government has rather tried to crush the Catholic spirit, and to sever the people from the priesthood. This is strikingly illustrated in the action during the last half-century regarding the question of education. The Irish nation has always cherished a love of knowledge; even in the hardest times of trial the lamp of learning has never been extinguished. When the Relief Bill gave freedom of worship it would have been natural to allow this consuming thirst of knowledge the means of being satisfied. The Government offered a system of non-Catholic and Godless education; but a nation whose children in the famine of 1848 had on many occasions calmly refused, while death was staring them in the face, to take the tempting food offered on condition of sacrificing their religious convictions, preferring death to loss of faith, was not the nation to accept education severed from religion. The people gathered their scanty resources, drew together distinguished scholars from England and other lands, as well as from their own, and spent some 40,000*l*. on the foundation of a Catholic University. But all in vain did the bishops plead and the people petition for a charter and for support for this University. Benefits which had been accorded to the Catholics of Canada and of Malta were refused to those of Ireland. Better by far that the British tax-payer's money should have been spent in founding this Catholic seat of learning, a boon for the great majority of the nation, a lasting institution of peace and order for the whole country, than that the money should be devoted, as has been the case for months past, to the sad necessity of supporting an armed force to suppress lawlessness.

'For God and Church and country' is the cry of the Irish nation. No people have ever loved the faith more; no people can be more attached to their country than are the Irish to the soil of their Emerald Isle; but the grasp of an iron hand has prevented the development of its resources, and kept its own people from possessing it. 'Such,'[1] says Bancroft, 'was the Ireland of the Irish, a conquered people, whom the victors delighted to trample upon and did not fear to provoke. Their industry within the kingdom was prohibited or repressed by law, and they were calumniated as idle. Their savings could not be invested in trade, manufactures, or real property, and they were called improvident. The gates of learning were shut on them, and they were described as ignorant.' The long story of the wholesale confiscations under Queen Elizabeth, James I., Charles I., Cromwell, and William of Orange is too terrible to repeat. To regain ownership of the land was impossible to the Irish Catholic; he was disqualified by law, which, however, in the interest of the landlord, permitted him to become a tenant. In this

---

[1] *History of United States*, vol. v. chap. iv.

position, being of a despised race, of a religion stigmatised by England as idolatrous, the tenant was treated heartlessly and inhumanly. It would be almost impossible to believe the descriptions of the wretchedness and misery left by different writers, were it not that they are too sadly supported by the accounts given during the past year by many special commissioners of the English press. To go back to the days of Dean Swift, writing of some of the better class of tenants, he uses these words : 'The families of farmers who pay great rents live in filth and nastiness, upon buttermilk and potatoes, without a shoe or stocking to their feet, or a house as convenient as an English hog-sty to receive them.' The famed Bishop Berkeley asks, 'Is there on the face of the earth any Christian and civilised people so destitute of everything as the mass of the people of Ireland?' and as lately as 1835 De Beaumont wrote : 'I have [1] seen the Indian in his forests and the negro in chains, and I thought in beholding their pitiable state that I saw the extreme of human misery ; but I did not then know the fate of poor Ireland. Like the Indian, the Irishman is poor and naked ; but he lives, unlike the savage, in the midst of a society which revels in luxury and adores wealth.' However disagreeable it may be to hear it, the combined testimony of writers of every century and of travellers of different countries compels the belief that the people of Ireland have had to slave oftentimes for landlords who in many instances have been aliens and absentees, and whose exactions and tyranny so ground down the tenants and labourers that the people were housed in cabins into which an Englishman would not put a favourite animal ; their nakedness was scarcely covered, their food was insufficient, and, depressed by suffering,

[1] *L'Irlande, Sociale, Politique et Religieuse,* tom. i. p. 222.

they were bereft of every laudable ambition and the sense of dignity which even moderately remunerated labour produces. In common justice it has to be added that there have ever been a large number of landlords who have realised and fulfilled their duties towards their tenants and have won for themselves the lasting affection of their people, and this number has been steadily increasing during the past fifty years. Ireland's second curse has been the system of Land Tenure; and in the change which must necessarily take place, it would be deplorable were the Government not to make fair compensation to landlords, many of whom will otherwise suffer grave injustice.

No wonder that a much suffering people should so often have risen and tried to shake off the alien yoke. Would not Englishmen and Scotchmen do in like manner? No wonder that with memories of such cruelty and injustice during many centuries agitators should raise a 'no rent' cry, which unhappily swamps the 'fair rent' provisions of the Land Act, and rouses a quick and sensitive people with the hope held out to them that once and for all they will be ridded of landlordism and freed from the government which, in their minds, is associated with the tyranny under which they have suffered.

Referring to the Irish Rebellion in 1793, Froude says: 'The long [1] era of misgovernment had ripened at last for the harvest. Rarely, since the inhabitants of the earth have formed themselves into civilised communities, had any country suffered from such a complication of neglect and ill-usage. The Irish people clamoured against government, and their real wrong from first to last had been that there was no government over them; that under changing forms the

[1] *The English in Ireland,* vol. iii. p. 348.

universal rule among them for four centuries had been the tyranny of the strong over the weak ; that from the catalogue of virtues demanded of those who exercised authority over their fellow-men the word justice had been blotted out. Anarchy had borne its fruits.' And since that period, the mind of the populace has been perpetually excited and bewildered by the impracticable idea of Ireland's absolute independence. That she needs increased facilities and less expensive means for the settlement of her own domestic concerns is conceded on every side. That her craving for an extension of self-government is just and legitimate, few will deny. Why, then, not apply to Ireland, without prejudice to the Empire's general interests, and making due allowance for difference of circumstances, the principle which has been productive of such happy results in Canada? At the commencement of Her Majesty's reign the Canadians were in revolt, and were a source of great anxiety to the British Government. The Earl of Durham recommended that the Dominion should have its own responsible Government, and that Canada should virtually be made master of its own domestic concerns. This nobleman was appointed High Commissioner, and his administration furnishes remarkable proof of the happy results of a policy based on solid principles, and in its action combining firmness and conciliation. No portion of the empire has manifested truer loyalty towards the Crown. This loyalty was warmly manifested on the occasion of the Prince of Wales's visit in 1860 ; and again, when it was feared that the mother country might be involved in war with Russia, by the announcement that Canada was willing to send a military contingent to take part in the campaign. Last November, at the convention of Liberal-Conservatives held in Toronto, it was unanimously resolved by the

1,400 assembled delegates 'that it is of the utmost importance to the Dominion that its connection with Great Britain should be kept up.'

A similar state of feeling might prevail in Ireland. By nature Irishmen love 'the quality'; they have always been glad to show loyal honour to royalty on the rare occasions when a sovereign or a prince of the blood has visited Ireland. In 1821 George IV. arrived in Dublin, and was received with every demonstration of loyalty. The air was rent with the acclamations of the multitude, who declared that he was the first English sovereign who had landed on their shores without hostile intentions. So struck was the king by his reception, that Lord Sidmouth was commanded to convey the following message : 'The testimonies of dutiful and affectionate attachment which his Majesty has received from all classes and descriptions of his Irish subjects have made the deepest impression on his mind, and he looks forward to the period when he shall re-visit them with the strongest feelings of satisfaction. His Majesty trusts that in the meantime not only the spirit of loyal union, which now so generally exists, will remain unabated and unimpaired, but that every cause of irritation will be avoided and discountenanced, mutual forbearance and goodwill observed and encouraged, and a security be thus afforded for a continuance of that concord among themselves which is not less essential to his Majesty's happiness than to their own.' Of the living members of the Royal Family, her Majesty the Queen, their Royal Highnesses the Prince and Princess of Wales, and the Duke of Connaught, know the warmth of welcome with which they have been received in Ireland. It is a great misfortune that a royal residence has never been established in Ireland, or a son of the sovereign held the office of Viceroy. By either of these measures loyalty might have been elicited and promoted, and absentee landlords induced to have their homes in the country.

And of Irish loyalty to the English Nation, the words of Froude are sufficient testimony:—' Strike the names of Irishmen from our own public life, and we lose the heroes of our proudest exploits—we lose the Wellesleys, the Pallisers, the Moores, the Eyres, the Cootes, the Napiers; we lose half the officers and half the privates who conquered India for us and fought our battles for us in the Peninsula. . . . What they can be even at home we know at this present hour, when, under exceptional discipline as police, they are at once the most sorely tempted and the most nobly faithful of British subjects.'

Let Ireland, then, be governed as a country with the large majority of the people Catholic ' before all things' ; let peasant proprietorship be permitted to increase and develop itself; let the labouring class receive a proper wage and be better housed; let every encouragement be given to the development of the national manufactures and resources of Ireland; let Royalty take some share in Irish public life; let landlords deal justly with their tenants as between man and man; let self-government be accorded to the fullest extent compatible with imperial interests—let these things be done, and Ireland will be a loyal, happy, prosperous country; energy and thrift and sobriety will then rapidly grow among the Irish people and disaffection and discontent will disappear; England's reproach will be taken away, and the stream of Irish emigration, which now bears with it ill-will against England and the desire of revenge, will, on the contrary, overflow with gratitude and blessings.

If it has dawned upon Government that Ireland is a

Catholic nation, with national aspirations and characteristics, and ought to be governed in accordance with Catholic ideas, then may the Government be congratulated for courageously turning Romewards and seeking the support of the fountain head of the spiritual authority of the Irish priesthood. It is the dawn of Ireland's glory, and of England's lasting peace with the Sister Isle. No more visible and striking proof that England is making a new departure in regard to Ireland could be given than the establishment of full diplomatic relations with Rome. Either of the great political parties effecting this will earn a special title to the gratitude of the Catholics of the whole Empire. And if Ireland's sorrows be the occasion of opening communications with the Sovereign Pontiff, then will Ireland have conferred on the Catholics of England yet one more favour, the complement of the Catholic Emancipation Act, which was won mainly through the griefs of Irishmen.

III.

The arguments which we have adduced in favour of the establishment of diplomatic relations between Great Britain and Rome have so far been drawn from the circumstances of the internal life of the British Empire. A glance at its external life will tend to strengthen the conviction of the expediency and importance of such relations.

The British throne is established in a capital which, geographically speaking, may be said to occupy the centre of the continental or land hemisphere; the British flag waves over nearly nine millions of square miles; under the sway of the British Sovereign there are, as already mentioned, some three hundred and three millions of human beings. In the Providence of God, the Saxon race, endowed with the power of organising and of ruling, has been enabled to create a Commonwealth greater than any other that has yet appeared on earth.

The principle of government in the British Empire differs from that in any other monarchy in the Old World, and is one with that of the United States of America. Our Government relies for its power, not on a military *régime*, but on the moral forces of obedience and respect for authority, of justice and liberty. Like the United States, but unlike the other European Governments, Great Britain strives to develop man, not merely as a fraction of the State, but as an integer, an individual, possessed of individual resources and responsibilities. This constitutes a fundamental difference, not only between England and other modern States, but between the English and the Roman Empire. In the latter the State was everything and the individual nothing; and Rome fell for lack of freemen, for lack of men who felt that they had personal rights and personal dignity to defend.

A similar spirit is manifested in the British Empire's relation with the rest of the world. Convinced that the final appeal of nations is to the God of armies, she has resources in reserve to support her in the fulfilment of her international duties, and to uphold her international rights. But under ordinary circumstances these resources serve for purposes of peace and of protection. By a strange anomaly this vast and scattered empire has a standing army of only some 160,000 men, yet the nations of the earth are convinced that abundant supplies of wealth and of men are at England's command, ready if there were an hour of need. Military supremacy is not England's ambition, her foreign policy is professedly by moral influences to uphold the cause of liberty and justice; and her alliances, offensive and defensive, are with nations which will follow the same course, and will not regard mere might as right.

Now, there is no kingdom more powerful or more in harmony with England's mind, as manifested in her foreign policy, than the Roman Catholic Church. She is conscious of her Divine birth, and of her Divine principle of life. She ever remembers the Divine promise which ensures her subsistence throughout all ages; and therefore the Church and her children have an abiding sense of her indestructibility; to Catholics it is a self-evident truth, and even to Protestants her power is manifest.

For Catholicism is more than a conviction or an individual sentiment, more than a school of religious thought, or an association for works of charity; it is rendered concrete by an organism. It is a perfect, public, visible society constituted in the form of a true kingdom, although spiritual in its order. It is the perfection of organism. Authority more than human compares it to the most perfect of all natural organisations, the human body. The Roman Church has distinct organs, each one with its own function; these organs are directed by one central motive power, and the whole frame is tempered so that every part contributes to the strength and life of every other part. From the Roman Pontiff, its centre, doctrinal and jurisdictional authority flow forth to every part of the world, and in return loving, willing obedience flows back even from the extremities of this body to Rome, which is its heart. The dogma of the Infallibility of the Pope has given new vigour and more precision to the belief of the faithful in the teaching authority of the Church, while the loss of the temporal power and the sufferings of the Holy Father have strengthened the bond of affection between the Pope and his children. God has allowed good to come from evil, and has thus confounded His enemies, for never was the Church in her episcopate and people more united with the Holy See. The Church stands before the world a mobilised army in the highest state of perfection.

Strong and indestructible as is the organism of the Roman Church, she has a yet greater source of strength in the gifts she offers to men, and in the nature of the sway which she exercises. Eternal, indestructible, and unchangeable truths are her gifts to men. She instils into the heart of childhood truth and justice, obedience and liberty, purity and self-restraint, and she reiterates the same lessons through life to old age. She proclaims a liberty which meets the deepest needs of human nature, and which is the foundation of all lasting social order. Civil and political freedom are of their very nature rather external than internal. Liberty of speech and action, the diffusion of power among the people, the limiting and controlling of governing power are the very elements of civil and political freedom. The spiritual freedom proclaimed by the Roman Church is of its very essence internal. It means the liberation of the intellect from ignorance, doubt, and error by means of Divine, and therefore absolute, truth; the liberation of the will from sensual appetites, passion, and malice. According to her teaching submission to truth is intellectual freedom; obedience to the moral law is moral freedom. Such teaching affects man's inmost being, becomes the solid foundation of social and spiritual life, and, being upheld by everlasting sanctions, rests on the surest and most solemn basis. Her work is of its nature the formation of the individual, and the consecration of individual freedom. In declaring all men to be equal before God, and in maintaining that each is an entire human being, with all the rights, dignity, and worth of an immortal soul endowed with a free will for the exercise of which it is responsible to its Creator, and also by asserting a law for all men above all human law, and binding on prince and people, the Church puts personal individuality on the noblest pedestal.

But while her doctrine and means of grace develop to the full individuality, her organic character and supernatural independent powers enable her to save in the natural order the individual from being absorbed by the State, or the State from being destroyed by the individual. She teaches the individual to regard the Divine origin of the power and authority of the State, and to render it loyal and conscientious obedience. She instructs the State, when need be, that its laws and its actions must be in conformity with the law of the King of kings, and raises her voice, repeating with the inspired writer : 'Hear, therefore, ye kings, and understand ; learn ye that are judges of the ends of the earth. Give ear you that rule the people and that please yourselves in multitudes of nations ; for power is given you by the Lord, and strength by the Most High, who will examine your works and search out your thoughts ; because, being ministers of His kingdom, you have not judged rightly, nor kept the law of justice, nor walked according to the will of God. Horribly and speedily will He appear to you, for a most severe judgment shall be for them that bear rule. For to him that is little, mercy is granted ; but the mighty shall be mightily tormented.'[1]

Again, the past history of the Church renders the most striking testimony to her power. She has been tried, and has ever proved invincible and victorious. Born lowly and despised, she triumphed over the whole might of the Roman Empire and pagan persecution,

[1] Wisd. vi. 2-7.

cast down the idols of the Gentiles, planted Christianity permanently in the city of the Cæsars, and restored to man the individuality which had been absorbed by the State.

Barbarians seated themselves in the ruins of the Roman Empire, invasion followed invasion, society was filled with disorders and was threatened with dissolution. The sole power of resistance to this storm, the sole salvation of Europe, was the Roman Church. She tamed and civilised the fierce barbarians by converting them to the Gospel, little by little she destroyed slavery, she raised woman to her true dignity, and brought to its just stature the individualism of the barbarian by the influence of her own strong and permanent central authority. Thus she introduced an enlightened sense of right and justice among the Governments of Europe, checked the violence of turbulent princes and fierce warriors, ameliorated manners and inculcated peace. The nations showed their gratitude by raising the Pope to the position of an earthly king, a Father among Christian princes. The ordinary law of the Church became the public law of Europe, and sovereigns and people appealed to the Sovereign Pontiff as final judge in things earthly as well as in things spiritual.

What the nations were pleased to give was rudely taken away. Since those days the Church has been assailed in varied ways, sometimes by her own children, sometimes by strangers, but her foundations could never be shaken. She is now, as she always has been and ever will be, the vivifying fountain of wisdom, of law, and of order for individuals and States—the only conservative, immutable power amidst the changes of nations.

This is the kingdom, strong in its origin, in its organisation, in its past successes, in the spiritual forces at its disposal, with which Great Britain ought, we maintain, to hold close alliance.

In 1848 the Marquis of Lansdowne introduced into the House of Lords a bill for the purpose of establishing relations with the Court of Rome. His Lordship showed that the Acts for settling the succession to the Crown were directed against spiritual and ecclesiastical reconciliation with Rome, but did not debar the Sovereign of England from establishing diplomatic relations, and that consequently to do so was perfectly legal, and that the experience of the world has proved such relations to be essential for political and temporal purposes. The noble Lord pointed out that the Kings of the line of Hanover had frequent communications with the Pope, notably during the Premiership of Sir Robert Walpole. He also drew attention to the fact that the Protestant State of Hanover established relations with Rome, by whose means England held her communications; that, at the commencement of the French Revolution, it was found expedient to have repeated communications with the Roman Pontiff, and that they were carried on through Sir John Cox Hippisley, M.P.; again, that when Lord Hood, in the Mediterranean, was in want of water, and referred to the Home Government regarding an application to the Pope, Burke, whose opinion was asked, wrote in the following terms, under date Oct. 3, 1793: 'Nobody can be so squeamish as to refuse benefits (nothing else will be offered by His Holiness) because they come from the Pope. . . . I confess I would, if the matter rested with me, enter into much more distinct and avowed political connections with the Court of Rome than hitherto we have had. If we decline them the bigotry will be on our part, and not on that of His Holiness. Some mischief has happened, and much good has, I am convinced, been prevented by our unnatural alienation. If the present state of the world has not taught us better things, our error is very much our fault.' The Marquis of Lansdowne also observed that the late Duke of Portland had entered into communication with the Court of Rome, for the laudable purpose of establishing Christianity in the Island of San Domingo, and had expressed his high sense of gratitude at the conduct of the Pope, and further, that by the Treaty of Vienna, in which England was a contracting party, the temporal rights of the Holy See were guaranteed under the Seal of the Sovereign of Great Britain.

The bill passed both Houses by considerable majorities, and met with popular favour, if we may judge by the liberal support given to it by the press as it passed through its several stages in Parliament. Unfortunately an amendment was inserted, to the effect that an ecclesiastic could not be received by England as ambassador from the Pope. As Lord Shrewsbury remarked, diplomatic relations cannot be established with any State except on terms of perfect reciprocity, and if her Majesty refused to receive an ecclesiastic as Minister from Rome, the Pope in his turn might fairly refuse to receive a Protestant. This reasoning is perfectly just, and indeed we may add that it would be offensive if her Majesty were to insist that the representative of the Ottoman Empire should not be a Mussulman, or that of the Celestial Empire other than a 'Heathen Chinee.' Common sense says that an ecclesiastic would best represent the mind of the Curia.

In the thirty years that have gone by since the introduction of Lord Lansdowne's bill, prejudice has almost disappeared, and there is every reason to hope that, were public opinion again sounded, the establishing of diplomatic relations with Rome would be still more emphatically accepted. The Pope is no longer possessed of temporal power; this, painful though it be, is but an accident. He was temporal King because he was

Sovereign Pontiff. Since the so-called Reformation the temporal possession of the Pope has been the necessary means of his spiritual independence; before the Reformation the Pope had in addition, by the concession of the Christian nations, an earthly kingship.

The civilised nations are threatened by a formidable enemy whose object is to destroy the present social basis and substitute another. The flood-gates of revolution opened in 1789 let loose the pent-up aspirations and cravings of the many who had long suffered oppression and despotism by the aggrandisement of royal authority, and at the hands of the 'privilégiés.' In the ears of such sufferers 'Liberty, Fraternity, Equality' were sweet music. Had the instigators of the revolution limited themselves to attacking old systems of government, to demanding radical changes in the institutions, laws, manners, and customs of their country; had they laboured to popularise government, to mitigate penal codes, to redress political and social grievances, to elevate and develop the poorer classes, France and Europe could only have benefited. Unfortunately the beneficent character of the movement was soon changed, and instead of reforming abuses it was directed against the very foundations of social order. Religion was dethroned, and reason was seated in her chair. Power was then said to come not of God, but of the people, and so it lost its sacred character; property was regarded as theft. This was followed by hatred of religion, by a denial of the supernatural, of the immortality of the soul, of everlasting reward and punishment, and of God Himself. Christianity in any form could in such a system have no existence, and men were thrown back into materialism, or at the best rationalism.

Societies were formed, having most elaborate and far-reaching organisations, to spread these ideas and to impart to them force by universal co-operation. Their strength and their effect may be judged by the authenticated deeds of Communism and Nihilism on the one hand, and by the growth of Internationalism and Socialism on the other. They ignore nationalities, and their network is spread over every civilised land. They defy the most vigilant secret police, and carry out their plans in spite of mighty battalions. The world was shocked by the assassination of the Czar, at whose word a million swords would have leaped from their scabbards; and Europe is even now wondering at the alarming rapidity with which Socialism, notwithstanding the iron rule of Bismarck, has developed its political vote in Germany, and is disturbing and embarrassing the politics of different nations.

Against such enemies the State is almost powerless. Force cannot eject or introduce ideas. Extensive secret operations, based on corrupted popular sympathy and having changeable centres of motive power, can easily elude the vigilance of the most efficient police. The Roman Church, and the Roman Church alone, can struggle effectively with these enemies. She is the Church of the poor, of the masses, to whom she makes known Christian Liberty, Christian Fraternity, Christian Equality. Her organisation, her teaching, her empire over individual consciences, the practical sense of personal responsibility to God which she generates, the sacred character she gives to authority: such are the arms which must make her victorious. And the signs of the times foreshow that the Roman Church, with her Divine vigour and vitality, will be the sole army in battle array against the organised forces of materialism and rationalism. She is unceasingly warning the nations that the divorce of religious training from secular instruction, and the ostracism of religion from the public affairs of men, must inevitably end in the destruction of social order. The Sovereign Pontiffs, as watchmen of the City of God, have, with the weight of their supreme authority, inculcated by their encyclical letters the true foundations of the most sacred patriotism. No more remarkable or valuable document of this nature exists than the letter of our Holy Father appended to this pamphlet.

It is therefore to the interest of each nation to have a loyal alliance with such a great world-wide moral force. Statesmen have tried to ignore it, and even to crush it; but they or their successors have seen the folly of such a policy. Now England of all kingdoms is the natural ally of the Roman Church. Both powers proclaim peace and liberty, obedience and respect for authority; in the extent of their rule and in their form of government they have much similitude; for the prosperity of each, perfect independence and the ebb and flow of free communication with the world are necessary; cordially united, they would do the greatest good to mankind by spreading law and order, and by stemming the tide of revolution.

Whether, then, we look to the well-being of so many millions of her Majesty's subjects who are Roman Catholics, or to the personal dignity which would be conferred on each Catholic subject by the honour paid to the Supreme Head of his Church, or to the full and perfect development which would be given to the moral and social influences of the Roman Church in the whole British Empire, or to the extension which might be given to Christianity among British heathen subjects, or to the immense support England's power would receive in fulfilling international duties, or to the help which might be given to stave off or reduce to a minimum the bane of that Socialism which is cankering other countries: it is of the greatest advantage that the Sovereign of England should hold Diplomatic Relations with the Sovereign Pontiff, the supreme Head of the Mother and Mistress of all Churches.

APPENDIX.

THE ENCYCLICAL LETTER[1] ('DIUTURNUM ILLUD')
OF OUR MOST HOLY LORD LEO XIII. BY DIVINE PROVIDENCE POPE TO ALL PATRIARCHS, PRIMATES, ARCHBISHOPS AND BISHOPS OF THE CATHOLIC WORLD HAVING GRACE AND COMMUNION WITH THE APOSTOLIC SEE.

To all Our Venerable Brethren the Patriarchs, Primates, Archbishops and Bishops of the Catholic World having Grace and Communion with the Apostolic See.

LEO PP. XIII.

VENERABLE BRETHREN,
HEALTH AND THE APOSTOLIC BENEDICTION.

THE long-continued and most bitter war waged against the Divine authority of the Church has reached that pitch whither it was tending; namely, to the common danger of human society, and especially of the civil power on which the public safety chiefly reposes. And in our own times most particularly this result is apparent. For popular passions now reject with more boldness than formerly every restraint of authority; and so great is the licence on all sides, so frequent are seditions and tumults, that not only is obedience frequently refused to those who rule States, but a sufficient safe guarantee of security does not seem to have been left to them. For a long time, indeed, pains have been taken to render rulers the object of contempt and hatred to the multitude, and the flames of envy thus excited having now burst forth, attempts have been

[1] This translation is taken from the *Tablet* of July 16, 1881.

several times made, at very short intervals, on the life of sovereign princes, either by secret plots or by open attacks. The whole of Europe was lately filled with horror at the horrible murder of a most powerful Emperor; and whilst the minds of men are still filled with astonishment at the magnitude of the crime, abandoned men do not fear to publicly utter threats and intimidations against other European princes.

These perils to commonwealths, which are before Our eyes, fill Us with grave anxiety, when We behold the security of princes and the tranquillity of empires, together with the safety of nations, put in peril almost from hour to hour. Nevertheless, the Divine power of the Christian religion has given birth to excellent principles of stability and order for the State, while at the same time it has penetrated into the customs and institutions of States. And of this power not the least nor last fruit is a just and wise proportion of mutual rights and duties in both princes and peoples. For in the precepts and examples of Christ Our Lord there is a wonderful force for restraining in their duty as much those who obey as those who rule, and for keeping between them that agreement which is most according to nature, and that, so to say, concord of wills, from which arises a course of administration which is tranquil and free from all disturbance. Wherefore, being, by the favour of God, entrusted with the government of the Catholic Church, and made the Guardian and the Interpreter of the doctrines of Christ, We judge that it belongs to Our jurisdiction, Venerable Brethren, publicly to set forth that which Catholic truth demands of every one in this sphere of duty; from which also it is made clear by what way and by what means measures may be taken for the public safety in so critical a state of affairs.

Although man, when excited by a certain arrogance and contumacy, has often striven to cast aside the reins of authority, he has nevertheless never been able to arrive at obeying no one. In every association and community of men necessity itself compels that some should have the pre-eminence; lest society, deprived of a prince or head, by which it is ruled, should come to dissolution and be prevented from attaining the end in favour of which it was created and instituted. But if it was not possible that political power should be removed from the midst of States, it is certain that men have used every art to take away its influence and to lessen its majesty, as was especially the case in the sixteenth century, when a fatal novelty of opinions infatuated so many. Since that epoch not only has the multitude striven that a liberty greater than is just should be meted out to it, but it has seen fit to fashion the origin and constitution of the civil society of men in accordance with its own will.

Indeed, very many men of more recent times, walking in the footsteps of those who in a former age assumed to themselves the name of philosophers, say that all power comes from the people; so that those who exercise it in the State do so not as their own, but as delegated to them by the people, and that, by this rule, it can be revoked by the will of the very people by whom it was delegated. But from these Catholics dissent, who affirm that the right to rule is from God, as from a natural and necessary principle.

But it is of importance to remark in this place that those who may be placed over the State may in certain cases be chosen by the will and decision of the multitude, without opposition to or impugning of the Catholic doctrine. And by this choice, in truth, the prince is designated, but the rights of princedom are not thereby conferred; nor is the authority delegated to him, but the person by whom it is to be exercised is determined upon.

There is no question here respecting forms of government, for there is no reason why the Church should not approve of the chief power being held by one man or by more, provided only it be just, and that it tend to the common advantage. Wherefore, so long as justice be respected, the people are not hindered from choosing for themselves that form of government which suits best either their own disposition, or the institutions and customs of their ancestors.

But as regards political power, that the Church rightly teaches comes from God, for it finds this clearly testified in the sacred Scriptures and in the monuments of antiquity; besides, no other doctrine can be conceived which is more agreeable to reason, or more in accord with the safety of both princes and peoples.

In truth, that the source of human power is in God the books of the Old Testament in very many places clearly establish. *By Me kings reign . . . . by Me princes rule, and the mighty decree justice.*[1] And in another place, *Give ear you that rule the people . . . . for power is given you of the Lord and strength by the Most High.*[2] And the same thing is contained in the Book of Ecclesiasticus: *Over every nation He hath set a ruler.*[3] These things, however, which they had learnt of God, by little and little men were untaught by heathen superstition, which as it has corrupted the true aspect and very many ideas of things, so also it has corrupted the natural form and beauty of the chief power. Afterwards, when the Christian Gospel shed its light, vanity yielded to truth, and that noble and Divine principle whence all authority flows began to shine forth. To the Roman Governor, ostentatiously pretending that he had the power of releasing and of condemning, our Lord Jesus Christ answered: *Thou shouldst not have any power against Me unless it were given thee from above.*[4] And St. Augustine, in explaining this passage, says: 'Let us learn what He said, which also He taught by His Apostle, that there is no power but of God.' The faithful voice of the Apostles, as an echo, repeats the doctrine and precepts of Jesus Christ. The teaching of Paul to the Romans, when subject to the authority of heathen princes, is lofty and full of gravity: *There is no power but from God,*[5] from which he draws this seemingly necessary conclusion: *The prince is the minister of God.*[6]

The Fathers of the Church have taken great care to proclaim and propagate this very doctrine in which they had been instructed. ' *We do not attribute,*' says St. Augustine, ' *the power of giving government and empires to any but the true God.*'[7] On the same passage St. John Chrysostom says: ' *In that there are kingdoms, and that some rule, while others are subject, and that none of these things are brought about*

---

[1] Prov. viii. 15, 16.   [2] Wisd. vi. 3, 4.   [3] Eccl. xvii. 14.
[4] John xix. 11.   [5] *Tract. civi in Ioan.* n. 5.   [6] Rom. xiii. 1, 4.
[7] *De Civ Dei,* lib. v. cap. 21.

by accident or rashly . . . . is, I say, a work of Divine wisdom.[1] The same truth is testified by St. Gregory the Great, saying: '*We confess that power is given from above to emperors and kings.*'[2] Verily the holy doctors have undertaken to illustrate also the same precepts by the natural light of reason in such a way that they must appear to be altogether right and true, even to those who follow reason for their sole guide. And indeed nature, or rather God who is the Author of nature, wills that man should live in a civil society; and this is clearly shown both by the faculty of language, the greatest medium of intercourse, and by numerous innate desires of the mind, and the many necessary things, and things of great importance, which solitary men cannot procure, and which they can procure when joined and associated with others. But now, a society can neither exist nor be conceived in which there is no one to govern the wills of individuals, in such a way as to make, as it were, one will out of many, and to impel them rightly and orderly to the common good; therefore God has willed that in a civil society there should be some to rule the multitude. And this also is a powerful argument, that those by whose authority the State is administered must be able so to compel the citizens to obedience, that it is clearly a sin in them not to obey. But no man has in himself or of himself the power of constraining the free will of others by fetters of authority of this kind. This power resides solely in God, the Creator and Legislator of all things; and it is necessary that those who exercise it should do it as having received it from God. *There is one Lawgiver and Judge, who is able to destroy and to deliver.*[3] And this is clearly seen in every kind of power. That that which resides in priests comes from God is so acknowledged that among all nations they are recognised as and called the ministers of God. In like manner the authority of fathers of families preserves a certain impressed image and form of the authority which is in God, *of whom all paternity in heaven and earth is named.*[4] But in this way different kinds of authority have between them wonderful resemblances, since whatever there is of government

---

[1] *In epist. ad Rom.* homil. xxiii. n. 1. [2] *Epist.* lib. ii. epist. 61.
[3] James iv. 12. [4] Ephes. iii. 15.

and authority, its origin is derived from one and the same Creator and Lord of the world, who is God.

Those who believe civil society to have arisen from the free consent of men, looking for the origin of its authority from the same source, say that each individual has given up something of his right, and that voluntarily every person has put himself into the power of that man in whose person the whole of those rights has been centred. But it is a great error not to see, what is manifest, that men, as they are not a nomad race, have been created, without their own free will, for a natural community of life; and besides that the agreement which they allege is openly a falsehood and a fiction, and has no authority to confer on political power such great force, dignity, and firmness as the safety of the State and the common good of the citizens require. But then only will the princedom have all those ornaments and guarantees, when it is understood to emanate from God as its august and most sacred Source.

And than this opinion it is impossible that any should be found not only more true but even more advantageous. For the authority of the rulers of a State, if it be a certain communication of Divine power, for this very reason immediately acquires a dignity greater than human: not, indeed, that impious and most absurd dignity sometimes desired by heathen emperors when affecting Divine honours, but a true and solid one, and one received by a certain Divine gift and benefaction. Whence it will behove citizens to submit themselves and to be obedient to princes, as to God, not so much through fear of punishment, as through respect for their majesty, nor for the sake of pleasing, but through conscience of doing their duty. And by this means authority will remain far more firmly seated in its place. For the citizens, perceiving the force of this duty, would necessarily avoid dishonesty and contumacy, because they must be persuaded that they who resist State authority resist the Divine will; that they who refuse honour to princes refuse it to God Himself.

This doctrine the Apostle Paul particularly inculcated on the Romans; to whom he wrote on the reverence to be entertained towards the higher powers with so great authority and weight that it seems that nothing could be prescribed more weightily.

Let every soul be subject to higher powers, for there is no power but from God, and those that are are ordained of God. Therefore he that resisteth the power resisteth the ordinance of God, and they that resist purchase to themselves damnation . . . . Wherefore be subject of necessity, not only for wrath, but also for conscience sake.[1] And in agreement with this is the celebrated declaration of Peter, the Prince of the Apostles, on the same subject. *Be ye subject, therefore, to every human creature for God's sake; whether it be to the king as excelling, or to governors, as sent by him for the punishment of evil-doers, and for the praise of the good, for so is the will of God.*[2]

The one only reason which men have for not obeying is when anything is demanded of them which is openly repugnant to the natural or the Divine law, for everything in which the law of nature or the will of God is violated it is equally unlawful to command and to do. If, therefore, it should happen to any one to be compelled to prefer one or the other, viz. to disregard either the commands of God or those of rulers, he must obey Jesus Christ, who commands us to *give to Cæsar the things that are Cæsar's, and to God the things that are God's*,[3] and must reply courageously, after the example of the Apostles, *We ought to obey God rather than men*.[4] And yet there is no reason why those who so behave themselves should be accused of refusing obedience; for if the will of rulers is opposed to the will and the laws of God, they themselves exceed the bounds of their own power and pervert justice; nor can their authority then be valid, which, when there is no justice, is null.

But in order that justice may be retained in government it is of the highest importance that those who rule States should understand that political power was not created for the advantage of any private individual; and that the administration of the State must be carried on to the profit of those who have been committed to their care, not to the profit of those to whom it has been committed. Let princes take example from the Most High God, by whom authority is given to them; and placing before themselves His model in governing the State, let them

[1] Rom. xiii. 1, 2, 3. [2] 1 Pet. ii. 13, 15. [3] Matt. xxii. 21.
[4] Acts v. 29.

rule over the people with equity and faithfulness, and let them add to that severity which is necessary a paternal charity. On this account they are warned in the oracles of the Sacred Scriptures, that they will have themselves some day to render an account to the King of kings and Lord of lords; if they shall fail in their duty, that it will not be possible for them in any way to escape the severity of God. *The Most High will examine your works and search out your thoughts: because being ministers of His kingdom you have not judged rightly. . . . Horribly and speedily will He appear to you, for a most severe judgment shall be for them that bear rule. . . . For God will not accept any man's person, neither will He stand in awe of any man's greatness; for He made the little and the great, and He hath equally care of all. But a greater punishment is ready for the more mighty.*[1]

And if these precepts protect the State, all cause or desire for seditions is removed; the honour and security of princes, the quiet and well-being of States, will be secure. The dignity also of the citizens is best provided for; for to them it has been permitted to retain even in obedience that greatness which conduces to the excellence of man. For they understand that, in the judgment of God, there is neither slave nor free man; that there is one Lord of all, rich *to all that call upon Him,*[2] but that they on this account submit to and obey their rulers, because these in a certain sort bring before them the image of God, *whom to serve is to reign.*

But the Church has always so acted that the Christian form of civil government may not only dwell in the minds of men, but that it may be exhibited also in the life and habits of nations. As long as there were at the helm of the State pagan emperors who were prevented by superstition from rising to that form of imperial government which we have sketched, she studied how to instil it into the minds of the peoples, who were bound, as soon as they had embraced the Christian institutions, to be desirous of bringing their lives into conformity with them. Therefore the pastors of souls, after the example of the Apostle Paul, were accustomed to teach the people with the utmost care and diligence *to be subject to princes and powers, to obey*

---

[1] Wisd. vi. 4, 5, 6, 8.   [2] Rom. x. 12.

at a word,¹ and to pray God for all men and particularly *for kings and all that are in a high station: for this is good and acceptable in the sight of God our Saviour*.² And the Christians of old left the most striking proofs of this; for when they were harassed in a very unjust and cruel way by pagan emperors, they nevertheless at no time omitted to conduct themselves obediently and submissively; so that, in fact, they seemed to vie with each other, those in cruelty, and these in obedience. This great modesty, this fixed determination to obey, was so well known that it could not be obscured by the calumny and malice of enemies. On this account those who were going to plead in public before the emperors for any persons bearing the Christian name, proved by this argument especially that it was unjust to enact laws against the Christians because they were in the sight of all men exemplary in bearing according to the laws. Athenagoras thus confidently addresses Marcus Aurelius Antoninus and Lucius Aurelius Commodus his son: '*You allow us, who commit no evil, yea, who demean ourselves the most piously and justly of all towards God and likewise towards your government, to be driven about, plundered, and exiled.*'³ In like manner Tertullian openly praises the Christians because they were the best and surest friends of all the empire: *The Christian is the enemy of no one, much less of the emperor, whom he knows to be appointed by God, and whom he must, therefore, of necessity love, reverence, and honour, and wish to be preserved together with the whole Roman Empire.*⁴ Nor did he hesitate to affirm, that, within the limits of the empire, the number of enemies was wont to diminish just in proportion as the number of Christians increased. There is also a remarkable testimony to the same point in the Epistle to Diognetus, which confirms the statement that the Christians at that period were not only in the habit of obeying the laws, but in every office they of their own accord did more, and more perfectly, than they were required to do by the laws. ' Christians observe these things which have obtained the sanction of the law, and in the character of their lives they even go beyond the law.' The

---

¹ Tit. iii. 1.   ² 1 Tim. ii. 1–3.   ³ *Legat. pro Christianis.*
⁴ *Apolog.* n. 35.

case, indeed, was different when they were ordered by the edicts of emperors and the threats of prætors to abandon the Christian faith or in any way fail in their duty; at these times, undoubtedly, they preferred to displease men rather than God. Yet even under these circumstances they were so far from doing anything seditious or despising the Imperial Majesty, that they took it on themselves only to profess themselves Christians, and declare that they would not in any way alter their faith. But they had no thought of resistance; calmly and joyfully they went to the torture of the rack, in so much that the magnitude of the torments gave place to their magnitude of mind. During the same period the force of Christian principles was observed in like manner in the army. For it was a mark of a Christian soldier to combine the greatest fortitude with the greatest attention to military discipline, and to add to nobility of mind immovable fidelity towards his prince. But if anything dishonourable was required of him—as, for instance, to break the laws of God, or to turn his sword against innocent disciples of Christ—then, indeed, he refused to execute the orders, yet in such wise that he would rather retire from the army and die for his religion than oppose the public authority by means of sedition and tumult.

But afterwards, when States had Christian princes, the Church insisted much more on testifying and preaching how much sanctity was inherent in the authority of rulers: from which it would follow that when the people thought of princedom, the image of a certain sacred majesty would present itself to their minds, by which they would be impelled to greater reverence and love of princes. And on this account she wisely provides that kings should commence their reign with the celebration of solemn rites; which, in the Old Testament, was appointed by Divine authority.

But from the time when the civil society of men, raised from the ruins of the Roman Empire, gave hope of its future Christian greatness, the Roman Pontiffs, by the institution of *The Holy Empire*, consecrated the political power in a wonderful manner. Greatly, indeed, was the authority of rulers ennobled; and it is not to be doubted that what was then instituted would always have been a very great gain, both to ecclesiastical and civil society, if princes and people had ever looked to the same object as the Church. And, indeed, tranquillity and a sufficient prosperity lasted so long as there was a friendly agreement between these two powers. If the people were turbulent, the Church was at once the mediator for peace; and recalling all to their duty, she subdued the more lawless passions, partly by kindness and partly by authority. So if, in ruling, princes erred in their government, she would go to them and, putting before them the rights, needs, and lawful wants of their people, would urge them to equity, mercy, and kindness. Whence it was often brought about that the dangers of civil wars and of tumults were stayed.

On the other hand, the theories of the body politic invented by late writers have already produced great ills amongst men, and it is to be feared that they will cause the very greatest disasters to posterity. For an unwillingness to attribute the right of ruling to God, as its author, is no less than a willingness to blot out the greatest splendour of political power and to destroy its force. And they who say that this power depends on the will of the people err in opinion first of all; then they place authority on too weak and unstable a foundation. For the popular passions, incited and goaded on by these opinions, will break out more insolently; and, with great harm to the common weal, descend headlong by an easy and smooth road to tumults and to open sedition. In truth, sudden uprisings and the boldest rebellions immediately followed in Germany the so-called Reformation, the authors and leaders of which, by their new doctrines, attacked from the very foundation religious and civil authority; and this with so fearful an outburst of civil war and with such slaughter, that there was scarcely any place free from tumult and bloodshed. From this heresy there arose in the last century the false philosophy, a new right as it is called, and a popular authority, together with an unbridled licence which many regard as the only true liberty. Hence we have reached the limit of horrors, to wit, Communism, Socialism, Nihilism, hideous deformities of the civil society of men and almost its ruin. And yet too many attempt to enlarge the scope of these evils, and under the pretext of helping the multitude, already have fanned no small flames of misery. The things we thus mention are neither unknown nor very far off.

This indeed is all the graver because rulers, in the midst of so great dangers, have no remedies sufficient to restore discipline and tranquillity. They supply themselves with the power of laws, and think to coerce, by the severity of their punishments, those who disturb their Governments. They are right to a certain extent, but yet should seriously consider that no power of punishment can be so great that it alone can preserve the State. For fear, as St. Thomas admirably teaches, *is a weak foundation; for those who are subdued by fear would, should an occasion arise in which they might hope for immunity, rise more eagerly against their rulers, in proportion to the extent of their restraint through fear.* And besides, *from too great fear many fall into despair; and despair drives men to attempt boldly to gain what they desire.*[1] That these things are so we see from experience. It is therefore necessary to seek a higher and more reliable reason for obedience, and to say explicitly that legal severity cannot be efficacious unless men are led on by duty, and moved by the salutary fear of God. But this is what religion can best ask of them, religion which by its power enters into the souls and bends the very wills of men, causing them not only to render obedience to their rulers, but also to show their affection and good will, which is in every society of men the best guardian of safety.

For this reason the Roman Pontiffs are to be regarded as having greatly served the public good, for they have ever endeavoured to break the turbulent and restless spirit of innovators, and have often warned men of the danger they are to civil society. In this respect we may worthily recall to mind the declaration of Clement VII. to Ferdinand, King of Bohemia and Hungary: *In the cause of faith your own dignity and advantage and that of other rulers is included, since the faith cannot be shaken without your authority being brought down, which has been most clearly shown in several instances.* In the same way the supreme forethought and courage of our predecessors have been shown, especially of Clement XI., Benedict XIV., and Leo XII., who, when in their day the

[1] *De Regim. Princip.* i. 1, cap. 10.

evil of vicious doctrine was more widely spreading, and the boldness of the sects was becoming greater, endeavoured by their authority to close the door against them. And We Ourselves have several times declared what great dangers are impending, and have pointed out the best ways of warding them off. To princes and other rulers of the State we have offered the protection of religion, and we have exhorted the people to make abundant use of the great benefits which the Church supplies. Our present object is to make princes understand that that protection which is stronger than any is again offered to them; and we earnestly exhort them in our Lord to defend religion, and to consult the interest of their States by giving that liberty to the Church which cannot be taken away without injury and ruin to the commonwealth. The Church of Christ indeed cannot be an object of suspicion to rulers, nor of hatred to the people; for it urges rulers to follow justice, and in nothing to decline from their duty, while at the same time it strengthens and in many ways supports their authority. All things that are of a civil nature the Church acknowledges and declares to be under the power and authority of the ruler; and in those things the judgment of which belongs for different reasons both to the sacred and the civil power the Church wishes that there should be harmony between the two, so that injurious contests may be avoided. As to what regards the people, the Church has been established for the salvation of all men, and has ever loved them as a mother. For the Church it is which, by the exercise of its charity, has given gentleness to the minds of men, kindness to their manners, and justice to their laws; and, never opposed to honest liberty, she has always detested a tyrant's rule. This custom which the Church has ever had of deserving well of mankind is notably expressed by St. Augustine when he says: *The Church teaches Kings to study the welfare of their people, and people to submit to their Kings, showing what is due to all, and that to all is due charity, and to no one injustice.*[1] For these reasons, Venerable Brethren, your work will be most useful and salutary if you employ with us every industry and effort which God has given to you in averting the dangers and evils of human

---

[1] *De morib. Eccl.* lib. i. cap. 80.

society. Strive with all possible care to make men understand and show forth in their lives what the Catholic Church teaches on government and the duty of obedience. Let the people be frequently urged by your authority and teaching to fly from the forbidden sects, to abhor all conspiracy, to have nothing to do with sedition, and let them understand that they who for God's sake obey their rulers render a reasonable service and a generous obedience. And as it is God *who gives safety to Kings*,[1] grants to the people *to rest in the beauty of peace and in the tabernacles of confidence and of wealthy repose*,[2] it is to Him that we must pray, beseeching Him to incline all minds to uprightness and truth, to calm angry passions, to restore the long-wished-for tranquillity to the world.

That we may pray with greater hope, let us take as our intercessors and protectors of our welfare the Virgin Mary, the Great Mother of God, the Help of Christians, and Protector of the human race; St. Joseph, her chaste spouse, in whose patronage the whole Church greatly trusts; and the princes of the Apostles, Peter and Paul, the guardians and protectors of the Christian name; and meanwhile, in token of the Divine favour, We most lovingly grant in our Lord to all of you, Venerable Brethren, to the clergy and people committed to your fidelity, Our Apostolic Benediction.

Given at Rome, at St. Peter's, on the 29th day of June, in the year 1881, the fourth year of our Pontificate.

Leo PP. XIII.

[1] Psal. cxliii. 11.   [2] Isai. xxxii. 18.

www.ingramcontent.com/pod-product-compliance
Lightning Source LLC
Chambersburg PA
CBHW022151090426
42742CB00010B/1473